CW00550094

POEMS

BY

DAVID DOWSON

www.daviddowson.com
www.daviddowson.co.uk
daraarts@sky.com

Acknowledgement

Special thanks to my mother, Beryl, who is always there for me and my sister, Jan Webber, author of the *Betty Illustrated* Children's books.

Edition One

www.daviddowson.com
www.daviddowson.co.uk

Other books also written
by David Dowson include:

Chess for Beginners
Chess for Beginners Edition 2
Into the Realm of Chess Calculation
Nursery Rhymes
The Path of a Chess Amateur
CHESS: The BEGINNER'S GUIDE eBook

Novels

Declon Five
Dangers Within
The Murder of Inspector Hine
Spooks Scarlett's Enigma
The Deception Unveiled
Webs of Blood and Shadows
Being Mini Lakshmi
Night Assassin
Cloak of Deception
Mini Lakshmi 31 Days in May
Poems
How to Write a Novel in Seven Days

A Christmas Poem

In the warmth of winter's embrace,
Where snowflakes softly dance with grace,
A message of love, peace, and joy,
To fill your heart, to bring you joy.

May Christmas' light, so pure and bright,
Guide you through the darkest night,
A beacon of hope, a gentle ray,
To light your path along the way.

Sending love, a gift so dear,
Wrapped in ribbons of hope and cheer,
May it find you where you stand,
And fill your days with love so grand.

Peace, like a gentle river's flow,
Calms your soul, helps you to grow,
Let it wash away each worry and fear,
And bring serenity, ever near.

And joy, like laughter's sweet refrain,
Echoing through your heart and brain,
May it lift you high, make your spirit soar,
With every day, forevermore.

So, let the spirit of Christmas reside,
Within your heart, let it abide,
And as the new year dawns anew,
May love, peace, and joy be with you.

For in this season, where hearts unite,
We find solace in the darkest night,
And though we may be far apart,
Love's connection binds our hearts.

So, let the love and peace and joy,
Of Christmas warm your soul, employ,
And may it stay with you each day,
Guiding you along life's precious way.

My Rose

She kissed me when we first met,
A moment in time I'll never forget.
Her lips, like petals soft and sweet,
In that instant, my heart skipped a beat.

A red rose I give to thee,
A symbol of love, pure and free.
Its crimson hue, a passionate flame,
An offering of affection without shame.

Together, we shall embark on a bold journey,
In this temple of love, our spirits unfold.
No constraints or boundaries shall we confine,
As our souls intertwine, transcending time.

In this vast expanse, our love shall grow,
It is unfolding secrets that only we shall know.
With each passing day, our bond will strengthen,
A testament to the love we have awakened.

Through mountains high and valleys low,
We'll traverse this world, our love on show.
Hand in hand, we'll face whatever may come,
For in each other, we've found our home.

In this verse, let our love be sung,
A symphony of emotions, forever young.
When she kissed me, my heart took flight,
Together, we'll soar in love's eternal light.

Whispers and Lies

Why, oh why, can't I reach the sky?

Determination and effort before it passes me by.

No time to sit or stand and cry.

May I find a way to ascend to the sky?

As I gaze at the towering skyscrapers above,

I can't help but feel the loss of love.

This city, filled with secrets and lies,

Yet I refuse to be halted from reaching the skies.

It won't be easy, the path to success.

This world paved with deceit, danger, and death.

One wrong move could mean a downfall,

But that's no problem, no problem at all.

The Meaning

Reaching for the Sky Amidst Steel and Stone,

In this concrete jungle,

I stand tall, proud, and alone.

My spirit unbroken,

My will unbound.

I reach for the sky,

Though the buildings crowd,

Their steel and stone exteriors,

A formidable sound.

The wind whispers secrets of those who came before,

Their struggles and triumphs,

Forever more.

Their footsteps echo through these city streets,

A testament to perseverance,

Sweet retreats.

The path ahead is fraught with danger and strife,

But I am not deterred,

My heart full of life.

For every obstacle,

I find a way to thrive,

And rise above,

Like a phoenix from the drive.

The sun sets slow and paints the sky with gold,

As I stand here,

My dreams unfold.

I know that tomorrow brings new tests and trials,

But I am ready,

Armed with courage and laughter,

No failures.

So let the skyscrapers reach for the heavens high,

I'll reach for mine and touch the sky.

In this concrete jungle,

Where shadows play and lights gleam bright,

A world of secrets hides,

Veiled from sight.

Lies whispered in alleys,

Truths concealed with art,

A labyrinthine web of deceit,

Entwining hearts.

But I am not deterred,

My spirit unbroken,

For in every shadow,

Hope is spoken.

I search for answers,

Through streets that wind,

And find solace in the beauty of the mind.

The city pulsates with life,

Its beat a symphony,

A melody of dreams,

A chorus of humanity.

Among the towering skyscrapers,

I stand tall,

Unfazed by the complexity of it all.

Secrets and lies may cloud the urban sky,

Yet within me burns a fire,

Never to die.

With each step forward,

I illuminate the night,

Chasing truth and justice,

With all my might.

So let the city's secrets remain untold,

For in their depths,

I've found a story bold.

A tale of resilience, strength, and grace,

That echoes through the concrete place.

With every step I take,

I face life's challenges anew,

No problems in my path,

Just opportunities to pursue.

I stand tall and strong,

My heart full of cheer,

Ready to tackle anything,

Without fear or doubt or sigh.

No problem at all,

No obstacle too great,

My willpower and determination can't be beat.

I forge ahead with courage in my soul,

Never backing down, never feeling control.

For when I say "no problem," it means so much more,

It signifies my readiness to explore.

To conquer each challenge,

To break through the mold,

And rise above,

With strength untold.

So bring on the test,

Bring on the fire,

I'll meet them head-on,

With desire.

No problem at all,

No issue too grand,

I'm ready to take on this world,

Hand in hand.

Stand and Shout

In days of yore, when youthful vigour glowed,

I thought fortune's hand would always shower

Blessings upon my head, and life unfold,

A tapestry of joy, with every thread of gold.

But now, alas! The years have come and gone,

Time's dark winds have blown away the dawn.

Of youth's bright promise, leaving naught but shade

And the reflection of a faded bloom.

In this glass, where once a radiant face looked back,

Now dwindles the visage of age, wrinkled and black.

With lines of care and sorrow etched so deep,

That even smiles must struggle to escape.

Yet still, within this frame of silver hair

And eyes that dimly gleam like autumn stars,

There burns a spark of hope, a fierce desire

To live each day as if it were my last, and fire.

My heart with dreams, though they may never be

Realized on earth, yet still they set me free.

From the prison of regret and wistful sighs

And guide me through these twilight years of life.

In youthful days of innocence and grace,

I thought the world a kinder place,

Where virtue and merit won the race,

And good fortune smiled upon my face.

But time has taught me otherwise, alas,

That life is not so fair and bright.

Good things don't simply drop from the sky,

And evil often takes flight.

For though I strove to do what's right,

To help and love as best I could,

I found that fate can play such tricks,

And luck can be oh so cruel.

Now I know that life's a test,

A trial by fire and flame,

Where strength and courage must be proven,

And only then will fame.

Though I may still hold on to dreams,

Of happiness and endless bliss,

I'll learn to fight for what I want,

And never let life's twists and turns dismiss.

In fields of war, I've fought for what is right,

My armour battered, my shield in flight.

With every blow, my heart beats strong and true,

For justice and peace, I fight anew.

The scars upon my skin tell tales of strife,

Each one a reminder of a life.

A life that could have been but wasn't mine,

Cut short by fate or so divine.

But still, I stand, through rain and shine,

Undeterred by wounds that never heal.

For though my flesh may bear the brunt,

My spirit remains unbroken, unsealed.

And when at last my time on earth is done,

I'll leave behind a legacy, won.

For I have fought for love, for freedom too,

And all that's good, I've fought to do.

In fields of carnage, where death reigns supreme,

I've seen the worst of humanity's darkest scheme.

The cries of the fallen, the stench of decay

Haunting my mind, day after day.

The screams of agony, the pleas for mercy

Echo through my soul, like an endless reverberation.

The smell of blood, the taste of fear

Linger in my senses, year by year.

The memories of battles lost and won

Forever etched in my mind, never undone.

The images of death, the sounds of pain

Harrowing reminders of what I've gained.

But though I may have survived the fray,

My heart and mind bear the weight of war each day.

The horrors I've witnessed, they will not fade,

A constant presence forever displayed.

In the glow of the flames, our hearts find solace and peace
As memories of days past bring smiles to our faces.
We sit around the hearth, a band of brothers true
Our bond forged in battle, strengthened by time and fate.

The crackle of the fire echoes our joyful shouts
As we raise our mugs in a toast to love and loyalty.
For though we may have fought on different sides,
Here, by the fire, we find common ground and unity.

The warmth from the flames wraps us in its tender hold
A comforting embrace that never grows old.
It's here, surrounded by the ones we trust
That we find the courage to face whatever comes next.

So let us cherish these moments, dear friends

And hold them close to our hearts until the end.

For they are the foundation upon which we build our lives

And the warmth of the fire will always be our guide.

Oh, the joys of culinary delight!

Our bellies warm, our hearts take flight.

In this place, we find peaceful reprieve

From battles fought, from lives lived brief.

Roasted meats and savoury stews

Cooked over an open flame, oh how they succulently do

Bring us together in fellowship true

As friends, united, our bond renew.

With each bite, our spirits soar high

We laugh, we toast, we dance, we sigh.

For in these moments, we forget our plight

And all is well, all is right.

So let us raise our glasses high

To friendship, love, and food that lies

Before us, a banquet of delight

A feast fit for heroes, shining bright.

In twilight hues of calm and quiet grace,

A fleeting respite from war's embrace,

We find ourselves within a fragile space,

Where hope and fear entwined do take their place.

The sun sets slow, its fiery glow fades fast,

Leaving night's dark veil to shroud our past.

And though our hearts may momentarily cease,

To beat with anxiety and endless unease.

For in this brief reprieve from mortal strife,

We sense the looming threat of life and death's strife,

Lurking in the shadows, waiting to pounce,

And tear apart the tenuous thread of truce.

So let us cherish these moments of stillness,

These flecks of time where love doth reign supremely,

For soon the drums of war shall sound once more,

And shatter forevermore this fragile score.

In this fleeting world of ours, where shadows loom and fears assail,

We find solace in the bonds of brotherhood, a love that never fails.

For though the night may darken, and the tempest rage and howl,

Together we stand firm, like pillars of strength, unyielding and whole.

Our hearts beat as one, our spirits entwined,

A bond so strong it cannot be broken, a flame that burns divine.

For in each other's eyes we see the light, the hope that guides us through,

And in these moments shared, we find the courage to face what's true.

So let us cherish every second, every breath we take,

For time slips away like grains of sand, and memories we make.

Let us hold fast to joy, to laughter and to love,

For in the end, these are the things that lift us from above.

And when the storm clouds gather, and the winds do howl and moan,

We'll stand together, unbroken, our spirit made of stone.

For in the eye of the hurricane, we'll find our peaceful place,

Where love and friendship shelter us, and give us grace.

In fields of carnage, where death holds sway

Where blood soaks the earth, night and day.

I've witnessed mankind's darkest display

Of brutality, in every way.

The cries of the fallen, the stench of despair
Haunt me still, like an endless prayer.
Echoes of pain, that never fade
A heavy burden, that weighs on my shade.

The screams of agony, the wails of doom
Resound within my soul, a funeral boom.
The howls of the damned, the groans of defeat
A chorus of sorrow, that cannot retreat.

Yet amidst the chaos, a glimmer of hope
A spark of resilience, a will to cope.
For even in darkness, there is light
A beacon of courage, that guides us through the fight.

In fields of glory, where heroes rise and fall,

I march towards victory, my spirit tall.

With every step, my heart beats strong and true,

For in each battle, I find a tale anew.

Through stormy skies and fierce engagements,

My courage holds fast, my spirit unbroken.

And though the fight may leave me worn and weary,

I know that in its wake, a story's born.

So let the battles rage on, for I know

That when all is said and done, I'll have tales to show.

Memories of bravery, of honour and might,

To cherish through the years, in the quiet night.

And when at last I lay my weapons down,

My body tired, but my spirit still renowned,

I'll sit by the fire, and share my stories bold,

Of conquests won, of foes defeated cold.

Then raise your glasses high, my friends so dear,

Let us toast to valour, to courage clear.

For though our bodies may bear scars and strife,

Our hearts remain unbreakable, rife with life.

Nightmares

In the dead of night,

I glimpse what induces a startling fright.

With ghouls, witches, and clowns in the eerie light,

Halloween emerges, a chilling sight.

Beneath the moon's pale, haunting glow,

A spectral scene unfolds with a sinister throw.

Ghouls with ghostly faces gleam,

Casting shadows like a twisted dream.

Witches cackle, broomsticks high,

Painting the sky with spells awry.

Sinister clowns with wide grins lurking in shadows,

Nowhere to hide.

In the midnight hour,

Fear takes flight as Halloween unfurls its fright.

The air thick with spooky delight,

A symphony of screams and laughter in the night.

Pumpkins flicker,

Their faces alight,

Carving tales of darkness and fright.

A chilling wind moans through the mist,

As skeletal trees creak and groan,

The graveyard whispers secrets untold,

Where restless spirits wander bold.

As the haunted hour weaves its maze,

The moon watches with a spectral gaze.

Yet, amidst the fright,

A thrill takes hold, a magical dance of young and old.

Costumes weave stories, a masquerade,

Where reality and fantasy cascade.

In the heart of darkness, a celebration bright,

Halloween's enchantment takes flight.

Justice

I stand before the Lord above,

With loss of love, angry and sad.

A longing heart gripped by grief,

Yet emotions won't consume me.

Here for purpose, seeking justice,

The Lord observes my feelings.

Will he grant the justice I seek?

Angry, sad, my love's now lost,

Yet my heart won't be overthrown.

For a reason, here I stand,

Justice sought in trembling hands.

The Lord gazes, knowing all,

Will retribution befall?

In this realm of life and death,

Where love and loss intertwine,

I stand before the Lord above,

Seeking justice, divine.

I once knew a love so sweet,

A bond that seemed eternal,

But fate had other plans for us,

And now it's all infernal.

Death, the cruel and relentless thief,

Stole my love away,

Leaving me here, heartbroken,

With sorrow in my sway.

But I refuse to be defeated,

By the hand of destiny,

I stand before the Lord above,

With a plea for clarity.

Anger courses through my veins,

Sorrow engulfs my soul,

But amidst the pain and darkness,

My purpose takes control.

For I am here not just for me,

But for all who've suffered loss,

To seek the justice that's deserved,

No matter the life's cost.

The Lord, the keeper of all truths,

His gaze is deep and wise,

He knows the depths of my despair,

The tears within my eyes.

Will he grant the justice I seek,

To a heart so broken and torn?

Or will he show me mercy,

And let my love be reborn?

In this epic quest for answers,

I stand firm, undeterred,

For love and justice are entwined,

By the power of the word.

So I plead before the Lord above,

With trembling hands and voice,

Grant me the solace I yearn for,

In this tumultuous choice.

For death may have stolen my love,

But love will never fade,

It lives within my beating heart,

A flame that will never shade.

And though I walk through shadowed paths,

With grief as my constant guide,

I know that love will conquer all,

With strength that won't subside.

So I stand before the Lord above,

With loss of love, angry and sad,

But within me burns a fire,

That no darkness can ever add.

And as I await the judgment,

In fields of gold, where wildflowers sway,

I hear the whispers of the Lord each day.

His wisdom guides me through life's fray,

And in His love, I find my way.

Through ashes and dust, I see the light,

A beacon shining bright and true.

For in the darkness, love takes flight,

And in His heart, I find my clue.

Death may loom, but love prevails,

And in the end, it never fails.

So let us walk together, hand in hand,

In this dance of life, on sacred land.

With every step, we'll find our way,

To brighter days, come what may.

For in the Lord's embrace, we'll stay,

And in His love, we'll find our way.

Old Oak Tree

In twilight's hush, beneath this ancient oak,

Whose boughs stretch far and wide, like Nature's cloak,

I sit and ponder on memories of days gone by,

When I was a child, my heart would dance with joyful sighs.

At three years old, I used to climb up high,

And rest upon a branch, feeling free and spry,

The world below, a blur of colours bright,

As sunbeams filtered through, in dappled light.

The gnarled bark whispers secrets of the past,

Of winter snows, spring showers, summer's warmth at last,

Each season leaves its mark so plain to see,

A living chronicle etched in history.

The wind caresses leaves, now golden brown,

Like autumn's embrace, before the cold descends down,

And as the trees stand bare, their limbs outstretched,

Their stories told, in every twist and wrinkle etched.

Oh, how I cherish these moments here,

With Nature's grandeur, so pure and clear,

For though the years have passed since last I played,

This oak still stands, unchanging, forever stayed.

I wander through its shade, my heart elated,

As memories of joyful days are relived,

When laughter echoed loud, and love was created,

In this sacred space, where time is forgiven.

The rustle of leaves, the chirping birdsong,

The gentle breeze that whispers sweet and long,

All blend together in perfect song,

To create a symphony of serenity.

And as I stand beneath this ancient tree,

I feel the weightlessness of history,

A sense of belonging to something more splendid.

So let me linger here, in this peaceful place,

Where Nature's beauty fills my soul with grace,

And though the world outside may rush and race,

Here, all is well, in this timeless embrace.

The Closing Toast

Dear brethren of the mystic tie,

As the night wanes fast.

Our work is done, our feast is o'er,

This toast must be the last.

Happy to meet, sorry to part,

Happy to meet again,

Our bond of friendship steadfast,

Forever it shall remain.

In this sacred realm, we gather,

Bound by secrets and solemn vow,

Our hearts entwined, forever linked,

In unity, we shall avow.

Through laughter shared and tears shed,

We've forged a bond so true,

A brotherhood that knows no end,

A kinship strong and new.

As we bid farewell for now,

Our spirits filled with cheer,

Our souls connected, intertwined,

In this grand cosmic sphere.

No earthly chain can match the strength,

That binds us heart to heart,

For we are bound by mystic ties,

That never shall depart.

Through whispered words and knowing glances,

Our secrets safely kept,

We find solace in this brotherhood,

Where trust and honour are adept.

From lodge to lodge, we journey on,

Seeking light in darkest night,

Guided by the compass of our souls,

Guided by truth's purest light.

Dear brethren, let us cherish now,

This momentary embrace,

For though we part, we're forever linked,

By love, by truth, by grace.

And as we go our separate ways,

Know this, my brethren dear,

Our bond shall stand, unyielding,

Through each passing month and year.

So let us raise our glasses high,

To friendship tried and true,

To brethren of the mystic tie,

To all, I raise my brew.

Cheers to the nights we've shared,

To the lessons we've been taught,

To the ties that bind us tightly,

To the love that can't be bought.

Dear brethren of the mystic tie,

As darkness turns to day,

Let's toast to our eternal bond,

As we go our separate way.

Dear brethren, let us raise a glass,

To memories that shall not fade,

To nights of revelry and joy,

In this mystic bond we've made.

Farewell, dear brethren, till we meet,
Again beneath the moonlit sky,
Our mystic tie unbroken,
Our spirits soaring high.

In this circle, we found solace,
A refuge from the world's demands,
United by a common purpose,
Bound by love that firmly stands.

With laughter as our secret code,
We danced and sang until the dawn,
The echoes of our mirth and cheer,
In these hallowed grounds, forever drawn.

Through whispered tales and sacred rites,

We wove a tapestry of dreams,

Our hearts entwined, forever bound,

In this realm where magic gleams.

But now, the time has come to part,

To wander on separate paths,

Yet, know our spirits still remain,

Deep within our hearts' own drafts.

So, raise your glass, dear brethren for this must be the last.

To moments cherished, never lost,

To friendships forged in fire and time,

To bonds that can't be tempest-tossed.

Farewell, dear brethren, till we meet again

Beneath the moonlit sky,

Our mystic tie unbroken,

Our spirits soaring high.

Dear brethren of the mystic tie,

The night is waning fast,

Our work is done O'er,

This toast must be the last.

Happy to meet, Sorry to part,

happy to meet again.

Masonic Ode

In twilight's hush, where shadows dance and play,

We gather here, in mystic fellowship array.

Our labours done, our feast now past its prime,

We raise this cup, to seal our bond divine.

With hearts full of joy, and spirits free,

We bid each other fond adieu, for now we must flee.

But though we part, our bond remains unbroken still,

To meet again anon, when next the moon doth fill.

Happy to meet, sad to part, yet grateful too,

For time spent together, in love and true devotion true.

So let us cherish memories of this merry night,

And hold them close, until our next delightful sight.

Mia

Mia lay so still,

Upon the velvet chair, her body's thrill.

No cares or woes did trouble her mind,

As peaceful dreams danced, her soul entwined.

Her eyelids closed, like petals of a flower,

Soft and delicate, without an hour.

She slept on, untroubled by any strife,

A vision of serenity, pure life.

With each breath, her chest rose high and low,

Like waves upon the ocean below.

And when she stirred, it was but to stretch,

And gaze around, her heart's gentle reach.

For all was well, no fear did stain,

Her spirit free from every strain.

And as she settled back into repose,

She knew that love and joy were hers to choose.

Mia sleeps soundly on the grey velvet chair,

Not a care in the world, not a worry to bear.

With eyes gently closed and whiskers at rest,

She dreams of adventures, both wild and blessed.

Nothing would faze her, nothing at all,

For Mia, the cat, stands tall and enthralled.

She dreams of moonlit dances on rooftops high,

And chasing the stars as they paint the sky.

Then, with a yawn, she awakens from her slumber,

Stretching her paws, she starts to remember,

That this cozy abode is her sanctuary,

A place of warmth, love, and endless serenity.

She looks around, with eyes bright and aware,

Knowing that all is safe and sound, without a single care.

The world outside may be chaotic and loud,

But within these walls, peace is allowed.

For Mia, the cat, finds solace and peace,

In this haven of comfort, where worries decrease.

She purrs with contentment, a soft melody,

A testament to her joy, so wild and free.

Oh, Mia, the cat, with your spirit untamed,

In the face of adversity, you're never constrained.

You remind us to find comfort in our own little space,

To embrace peaceful moments, to savor their grace.

So sleep, sweet Mia, on your grey velvet throne,

Your dreams a reminder that we all have our own.

And may we, like you, find solace profound,

In the haven of our hearts, where happiness is found

Schizophrenic

I hear the voices every minute of the day,
Whispering secrets that make my mind sway.
Visual hallucinations, they never go away,
Painting illusions in hues of grey.

Ordering me to do things against my moral compass,
Their words entwined, a web of pure chaos.
But I stand fast on a path that does not sway,
Defying their commands, come what may.

In this vast expanse of a troubled mind,
Where sanity and madness intertwine,
I grapple with shadows that dance and play,
Yet, I remain resilient, come what may.

For within me burns a flame, unwavering,
A core of strength that keeps me from wavering.
Though the voices persist, their whispers so loud,
I stand tall, unbowed, amidst the crowd.

They try to knock me off this chosen course,

To lead me astray, to unleash remorse.
But I won't succumb, won't let them prevail,
My spirit resilient, it shall not fail.

In the depths of darkness, I find my light,
A beacon of hope, burning ever so bright.
I navigate this labyrinth, strong and brave,
For I am determined, my soul to save.

So, let the voices murmur, let them speak,
For I shall rise above, my spirit unbreakable and unique.
In the face of adversity, I shall remain,
Defiant and resolute, my strength sustained.

For I hear the voices every minute of the day,
And visual hallucinations never go away.
But I stand firm, grounded in my way,
Embracing the challenge, come what may.

Truth No Lies

In words of wisdom, I do proclaim,

My speech is guided by virtue's name.

I speak no lies, I tell the truth.

With every word, my heart doth proof.

My tongue is pure, my mind is clear.

I speak not to deceive or fear.

But to uplift and bring us near.

To the beauty that we all hold dear.

In love and kindness, I do strive.

To heal the wounds that we all arrive.

And in these words, I hope you thrive.

For truth and love will never divide.

So listen well, and hear my voice.

I speak no lies, but only choice.

That brings us closer to our goal.

Of living life with love and soul.

Our Spirits Soar

In fields of green where truth is sown,

We plant the seeds of love profound.

Where words of kindness do abide.

And honesty our hearts doth pride.

Speak no lies, but only choose.

To voice the truth we hold anew.

For in the power of love we find.

Strength that binds all humankind.

With every word we utter true.

Our spirits soar and grow anew.

In harmony we stand as one.

United in our quest begun.

Through laughter and through tears we all share.

The journey of our lives we bear.

But with each step we take in faith.

Our bond of love will forever last.

So let us strive to live with grace.

And fill our days with love and light.

That in the end, we may embrace.

A life well lived, a soulful sight.

Blind

In twilight's hush, where shadows dance and play,

I wander lost, without a guiding ray.

My footsteps falter, night's veil does shroud,

And in the darkness, all is clouded proud.

The stars above, they twinkle bright and clear,

But their light fails to pierce the thickening fear.

For alone I cannot see, the world around,

Blinded by the night, my vision profound.

Yet, as the day breaks, and morning dew,

A new hope stirs, and my heart anew.

With every step, my spirits lift,

As dawn's embrace, my sight revives and rift.

But alas, the sun's warm touch, does not bring,

The clarity of sight, my soul would cling.

For in its glow, my vision still does fade,

And in the light, my blindness is displayed.

So here I stand, in this endless night,

Alone and lost, without a guiding light.

My senses dulled, my spirit weak,

And in the darkness, my fate to seek.

He Who Hesitates Loses

He who hesitates, his chances do lose

In the game of life, he'll find no rose

For indecision breeds doubt and fear

And opportunity slips away clear

But boldness and courage will win the day

With confidence, success will come what way

So seize the moment, don't delay

For he who hesitates will surely stray

And when the path ahead is unclear

Take action now, have no fear

For in the end, it's not the plan that matters

It's the courage to take the first step that clatters

So don't wait for the perfect time

Or let your doubts hold you back in line

Just move forward with all your might

For he who hesitates will surely lose the fight

In Twisted Alleys

In twisted alleys, where darkness reigns supreme,

Lurk sinister clowns, their grins so wide and gleaming.

With painted-on smiles, they dance and prance,

But beneath the makeup, evil intentions advance.

Their eyes glint menacingly in the night,

As they search for prey, with wicked delight.

They creep and slink, like shadows on the wall,

Leaving no trace of their presence at all.

Their laughter echoes through deserted streets,

A haunting sound that pierces hearts and seats.

It's a chilling melody, full of fear and dread,

That sends shivers down your spine, and makes you dread.

So watch out for these clowns with their wide grins,

For they may be hiding in plain sight within.

Their sinister intentions, you cannot divine,

And once they catch you,

there'll be no escape from their clime.

Smiles of the Clowns

In twisted alleys, where darkness reigns supreme,

Lurk sinister clowns, their grins so wide and gleaming.

With painted-on smiles, they dance and prance,

But beneath the makeup, evil intentions advance.

Their eyes glint menacingly in the night,

As they search for prey, with wicked delight.

They creep and slink like shadows on the wall,

Leaving no trace of their presence, no presence at all.

Their laughter echoes through deserted streets,

A haunting sound that pierces hearts and seats.

It's a chilling melody, full of fear and dread, and makes you dread.

So watch out for these clowns with their wide grins,

For they may be hiding in plain sight within.

But do not let fear consume your soul,

For there is courage within that can make you whole.

In the darkest corners, where nightmares thrive,

Unleash your strength. Let it come alive.

Stand tall against the darkness, with unwavering might,

Illuminate the shadows with your radiant light.

For in the twisted alleys, where evil roams,

There also exists the power to transform.

With empathy and kindness, let love lead the way,

And banish the darkness in which clowns now sway.

So fear not the laughter that echoes in the night,

For behind those masks lies the need for light.

Embrace your own power, let it shine supreme,

And in the face of evil, let goodness redeem.

Fields of Gold

In fields of gold, where wildflowers sway,

A gentle breeze whispers through the day,

Birds sing sweet melodies all night,

As lovers dance beneath the light.

The sun shines bright, its rays so bold,

Warming skin and lifting spirits cold,

The scent of blooms fills every fold,

A symphony of joy untold.

Oh, what a wondrous sight to see,

A summer's day, so full of glee,

The world awakened from its sleep,

To revel in this beauty deep.

So let us bask in the sun's embrace,

And chase away the morning dew,

For on this day, we find our grace,

In love, laughter, and all things new.

A summer's day, oh so bright and gay,

With sunshine warm and birds at play,

The breeze is sweet, the skies are blue,

A perfect time for me and you.

The flowers bloom in vibrant hues,

Their scent fills the air, so pure and true,

The trees sway gently in the breeze,

As if they danced to music's ease.

The world is alive, it seems,

In this season of joyous dreams,

So let us revel in its grace,

And fill our hearts with love and space.

Thou art more lovely and more temperate,

Rarely have we seen such beauty stay,

So let us cherish every moment, come what may.

In fields of green, where wildflowers sway,

Thy grace doth dance, like sunbeams play,

A vision rare, a sight to stay,

Thou art more lovely, in every way.

With eyes so bright, and hair so fair,

Thy smile doth light up the evening air,

So let us cherish each passing day,

And hold thee close, in every way.

For thou art more than just a dream,

More lovely still, than any theme,

Rarely have we seen such beauty stay,

So let us cherish every moment, come what may.

In Days of Yore

In days of yore, when life was new,

And dreams were bright, and hopes anew,

I soared on wings of pure delight,

Without a care, or any plight.

My heart was free to dance and sing,

Unshackled by the world's dark sting,

I chased each sunrise with gleeful grace,

And basked in love's warm, golden place.

But then, oh cruel fate! It came,

This soul that now doth hold me bound,

It cast its spell, and took my name,

Leaving naught but sorrow profound.

Now I am trapped within this cell,

A prisoner of this endless spell,

Longing for freedom, lost and gone,

Left to weep and mourn alone.

Oh, how I yearn for those sweet days,

When I could fly without dismay,

When laughter filled my heart and mind,

And joy did leave me blind.

But alas, those times are far away,

And here I stay, in endless gray,

A captive soul, forever bound,

By this prison of my own mind.

I yearn for the touch of gentle breeze,

To feel the warmth of sunlight's tease,

To taste the freedom that once was mine,

To break these chains, to truly shine.

Oh, how I ache for the vibrant hues,

Of life's palette, where dreams go lose,

To dance with joy in fields of gold,

And let my spirit once again unfold.

But in this darkness, I find a spark,

A glimmer of hope, a tiny remark,

For deep within, my spirit fights,

To reclaim the days of radiant lights.

Though time has worn my wings so thin,

And despair seems close to win,

I'll rise above these imprisoning walls,

And let my spirit's song resound in halls.

For even in this captive state,

I refuse to let my dreams abate,

I'll sing the songs of freedom's call,

And break the chains that hold me small.

In days to come, I'll soar once more,

With renewed purpose, my heart will soar,

For though this spell may try to claim,

My spirit's fire remains untamed.

So, hear my plea, oh universe vast,

Release me from this shadowy cast,

Restore my wings, let dreams take flight,

And set me free from this endless night.

Another Sunny Day

A summer's day, oh so bright and gay,

With sunshine warm and birds at play,

The breeze is sweet, the skies are blue,

A perfect time for me and you.

The flowers bloom in vibrant hues,

Their scent fills the air, so pure and true,

The trees sway gently in the breeze,

As if they danced to music's ease.

The world is alive, it seems,

In this season of joyous dreams,

So let us revel in its grace,

And fill our hearts with love and space.

Thou art more lovely and more temperate,

Rarely have we seen such beauty stay,

So let us cherish every moment, come what may.

In fields of green, where wildflowers sway,

Thy grace doth dance, like sunbeams play,

A vision rare, a sight to stay,

Thou art more lovely, in every way.

With eyes so bright, and hair so fair,

Thy smile doth light up the evening air,

So let us cherish each passing day,

And hold thee close, in every way.

For thou art more than just a dream,

More lovely still, than any theme,

Rarely have we seen such beauty stay,

So let us cherish every moment, come what may.

Summer's Day

A summer's day, so full of glee,

The world awakened from its sleep,

To revel in this beauty deep.

So let us bask in the sun's warm embrace,

Chasing away the morning dew's trace,

For on this day, we find our grace,

In love, laughter, and all things new.

In this vast expanse of golden hue,

Nature's canvas painted with a breath-taking view,

We wander through this tapestry divine,

Where beauty and serenity gracefully entwine.

Each wildflower, a stroke of vibrant grace,

Blooms freely, adorning this tranquil space,

Their colours dance, a symphony in flight,

Elevating the senses, igniting pure delight.

The breeze, a gentle whisper in our ears,

Caressing our souls, erasing all fears,

It carries the melodies of birds above,

Their songs echoing, filling us with love.

Underneath the radiant sun's tender embrace,

We surrender to its warmth, feeling its grace,

Its rays reach deep, touching our very core,

Awakening passion, igniting us to soar.

And as the day unfolds, we find our way,

In this symphony of light, living for today,

For in this moment, time stands still,

In fields of gold, where dreams fulfil.

So let us dance beneath the sun's bright gaze,

Swirling and twirling in its golden haze,

Embracing love, laughter, and all things new,

In this summer's day, where possibilities ensue.

In fields of gold, where wildflowers sway,

We become one with nature's grand display,

A testament to life's endless embrace. He Who Hesitates Loses

He who hesitates, loses the chance,

In life's game, a missed dance.

Indecision breeds doubt and fear,

Opportunity slips away, crystal clear.

Boldness and courage win the day,

With confidence, success finds its way.

Seize the moment, don't delay,

For hesitancy leads dreams astray.

When the path ahead is unclear,

Take action now, have no fear.

In the end, it's not the plan that clatters,

But the courage to take the first step that matters.

Don't wait for the perfect time,

Doubts shouldn't hold you back in line.

Move forward with all your might,

For he who hesitates will surely lose the fight.

Troubled Mind

Voices whisper every minute of the day,

Secrets weaving illusions, shades of gray.

Visual hallucinations that never stray,

Painting shadows in a mind's disarray.

They order actions against my moral thread,

Words entwined, chaos widespread.

Yet, I stand unwavering on this chosen sway,

Defying commands, resolute each day.

In a troubled mind where sanity collides,

I grapple with shadows that linger, bides.

Resilient, I face this disarray,

Holding strong, unyielding, come what may.

Within me burns a flame, steadfast and bright,

A core of strength, resisting the night.

Though voices persist, loud and proud,

I stand tall, unbowed, amidst the crowd.

They try to derail this chosen course,

Lead astray, unleash remorse.

Yet, I won't succumb, won't let them prevail,

My spirit unwavering, it shall not fail.

In the depths of darkness, I find my light,

A beacon of hope, burning ever so bright.

Navigating the labyrinth, strong and brave,

Determined, my soul to save.

Let the voices murmur, let them speak,

I rise above, spirit unbreakable, unique.

In adversity, I remain,

Defiant, resolute, strength sustained.

Voices linger every minute of the day,

Visual hallucinations never at bay.

Yet, I stand firm, grounded in my way,

Embracing the challenge, come what may.

In Times of Woe

In times of woe, when shadows loomed ahead,
A seed of doubt within my mind was bred.
So I took a different path, one less worn,
Along the branch of life, where few had been born.

The road was crooked, and treacherous to tread,
But I walked on, with courage in my stead.
For though the journey was hard and long,
I knew that growth would come, and a new song.
The trees above me whispered secrets old,
And the winds that blew were full of gold.
The flowers that bloomed were rare and bright,
And in their beauty, I found my light.
The world around me may have seemed dark,

But in myself, I found a spark.
A spark of hope, a flame of might,
That guided me through the endless night.
And though the path was fraught with strife,
I walked it bravely, with heart alive.
For in the end, I found a truth profound,

That even in darkness, there is still ground.
In slumber's embrace.

FEAR

In strength, I am a tower of might,

A fortress that stands through endless night.

My will is unbreakable, my spirit pure,

I am the one who will never succumb.

But weakness creeps in like a thief in the night,

And steals away my courage, leaving me tight.

My heart trembles, my knees grow weak,

And I feel myself lost, unable to speak.

Yet even in vulnerability, I find power,

For it is then that I can shower

Compassion and kindness upon all,

And lift them up from their darkest fall.

So though I may be mean as a bear,

Or nice as a lamb, I am always fair.

For within me resides both light and shade,

And I am the person no one can abrade.

As cool as ice, I face life's test,

With confidence and grace, I pass the rest.

I am strong, yet gentle as a breeze,

And in my heart, there is peace and ease.

FEAR 2

In strength, I am a tower of might,
A fortress that stands through endless night.
My will is unbreakable, my spirit pure,
I am the one who will never succumb.

But weakness creeps in like a thief in the night,
And steals away my courage, leaving me tight.
My heart trembles, my knees grow weak,
And I feel myself lost, unable to speak.

Yet even in vulnerability, I find power,
For it is then that I can shower
Compassion and kindness upon all,
And lift them up from their darkest fall.

So though I may be mean as a bear,
Or nice as a lamb, I am always fair.
For within me resides both light and shade,
And I am the person no one can abrade.

As cool as ice, I face life's test,
With confidence and grace, I pass the rest.
I am strong, yet gentle as a breeze,
And in my heart, there is peace and ease.

I stand tall, a titan of strength,
Embracing life's journey, no matter the length.

With every challenge, I grow and learn,
My spirit resilient, forever to yearn.

Like a mountain, unyielding and grand,
I withstand the storms with unwavering hand.
My foundation sturdy, my roots deeply set,
I rise above, never to forget.

But even in my towering might,
I embrace the darkness, the fragile light.
For it is in my weakness, my vulnerability,
That I find strength, my true ability.

In the depths of my soul, compassion resides,
A beacon of hope, where love collides.
I extend my hand to those in need,
A source of comfort, a friend indeed.

So judge me not by my fierce exterior,
For within beats a heart, compassionate and superior.
I am the embodiment of balance and grace,
A paradox, a masterpiece, in this vast space.

I am a tower of might, a fortress strong,
Yet gentle as a breeze, I dance along.
In my vulnerability, I find my power,
And in my heart, love will forever flower.

So let me be both fierce and kind,
A testament to the strength of the mind.

For in this world, where shadows roam,
I am the poem, finding strength in the unknown.

SPEED

In realms of shadow and darkness profound,

Where mortal eyes dare not venture around,

I dwell in secrecy unbound,

A fleeting presence hard to find.

My footsteps whisper on the air,

Soft as the rustle of silken hair,

Yet swift as lightning flashes bright,

Leaving naught but shadows in sight.

Though sought by many, never caught,

I dance within the veil of thought,

Ephemeral visions of delight,

Vanishing before the morning light.

For I am swifter far than sound,

Faster than any mortal bound,

And though you seek me night and day,

I shall forever slip away.

In realms of shadow and darkness profound,
Where mortal eyes dare not venture around,
I dwell in secrecy unbound,
A fleeting presence hard to find.

My footsteps whisper on the air,
Soft as the rustle of silken hair,
Yet swift as lightning flashes bright,
Leaving naught but shadows in sight.

Though sought by many, never caught,
I dance within the veil of thought,
Ephemeral visions of delight,
Vanishing before the morning light.

For I am swifter far than sound,
Faster than any mortal bound,
And though you seek me night and day,
I shall forever slip away.

In this tapestry of twilight's embrace,
I wander, unseen, in every space,
Like whispers carried on the wind,
I shall elude, ever unconfined.

Through the labyrinthine depths I glide,

Where echoes of forgotten dreams reside,
A phantom, elusive, beyond reach,
In the realm where secrets breach.

I am the dance of the midnight's hue,
A symphony of shadows, ever anew,
Unfathomable, an enigma untold,
In the vast expanse of mysteries unfold.

In the corners of your mind, I reside,
In the fleeting moments where thoughts collide,
A fleeting muse, ethereal and grand,
I slip through fingers like shifting sand.

Yet, fear not my elusiveness, dear friend,
For in the chase, a lesson I intend,
To seek the intangible, the unknown,
To cherish the fleeting beauty we've sown.

So, let your heart be the compass that guides,
Through the realms where darkness abides,
Embrace the whispers, the ever fleeting,
For in their passing, there's still a greeting.

In realms of shadow and darkness profound,
Where mortal eyes dare not venture around,
I am the essence that forever abounds,
A transient spirit, forever unbound.

BEATING THE BULLY

I am looked for yet cannot be found,
For I am faster than light or sound.
Through the vast expanse of time and space,
I roam, a phantom, leaving no trace.

In every corner of the universe,
My presence eludes, like a cosmic curse.
I dance with stars, their brilliant light,
But vanish swiftly, before day or night.

I am the whisper in the gentle breeze,
The fleeting shadow amid towering trees.
I am the thought that slips your mind,
The elusive answer you can never find.

I race with comets, streaking across the sky,
Leaving beholders wondering, asking why.
I am the blink of an eye, in a single beat,
Gone before you realize, a moment fleet.

Seek me in the echoes of distant cries,
In the shimmering tears that cloud your eyes.
But know, my seeker, I am beyond your grasp,
Too swift, too agile, too vast to clasp.

For I am time, the enigma of existence,
An intangible force, defying all resistance.
I am the eternal motion, forever in flight,
Unbound by boundaries, a constant delight.

Though I am elusive, slipping through your hands,
Embrace my essence, as the universe expands.
For in the quest to find what cannot be caught,
We discover the beauty of every fleeting thought.

TRIUMPH'S SO SWEET

Triumphs so sweet,
When I did beat,
The person with my hands and feet.

In this vast realm of endless strife,
Where battles rage with fervent might,
I stood alone, my soul alight,
Seeking triumph's golden light.

With every breath, strength surged anew,
A warrior's heart, bold and true,
I faced the challenge, no foe would subdue,
For victory's taste, I yearned to pursue.

Through countless hours of sweat and strain,
I honed my skills, dismissed the pain,
In the arena, a dance of grace,
I defied odds, my destiny to embrace.

With nimble steps and thunderous roar,
I fought my battles, to settle the score,
A symphony of motion, a mighty roar,
Triumph awaited, behind every door.

In the ring, my body soared,
A warrior unleashed, the crowd adored,
The rhythm of combat, a dance of might,

I fought with valour, through the darkest night.

Triumphs so sweet, they crowned my head,
A laurel wreath, by victory led,
But in my heart, humility spread,
For triumph's taste, it was never bred.

For true triumph lies beyond the fight,
In empathy's embrace, in love's pure light,
To lift others up, with all our might,
To celebrate their victories, burning bright.

So let us not be defined by our feats,
But by the kindness that our soul completes,
Triumphs so sweet, when compassion beats,
In unity, our victories shall meet.

In this vast realm where battles cease,
A triumph of love, a triumph of peace,
Let our hands and feet, forever entwined,
Forge a legacy, transcending time.

EMERALD AND DIAMONDS

I've got a story, a story to tell,
At a time when I was doing so well,
Emerald and diamonds, gold as well.
Cash was no problem. It flowed like water
over a waterfall. From ill-gotten assets.

In this vast realm of deceit and desire,
I swam in riches, fueled by the fire
Of ambition, consuming me whole,
Eager to possess, to control.

But as the embers of morality waned,
A haunting truth within me remained,
For wealth amassed by sinister means,
Leaves hollow hearts and shattered dreams.

The emerald's luster, once so bright,
Now masked in shadows, devoid of light,
Diamonds sparkling, but with no soul,
Their true worth lost in the pursuit of control.

The golden gleam that once held allure,
Became tarnished, a reflection impure,
For cash that cascaded, abundant and free,
Was tainted by the whispers of dishonesty.

Ill-gotten assets, ill-gotten gains,

An empire built on others' pains,
The truth concealed beneath a veneer,
Of opulence and power, fueled by fear.

Yet, as the facade began to crumble,
I saw the wreckage of my choices humble,
A realization, as clear as day,
That ill-gotten wealth could never repay.

For true riches lie not in material wealth,
But in a heart filled with love and health,
In kindness given and bridges built,
In the compassion that can never wilt.

So, I shed the shackles of my past,
Embracing a future that's built to last,
With newfound purpose and a story to share,
Of redemption sought, of lessons laid bare.

No longer defined by ill-gotten gain,
I choose a path where integrity reigns,
For in the end, it's the legacy we leave,
That truly determines what we receive.

So let us learn from this cautionary tale,
That chasing false riches will only fail,
For in our hearts, lies the true measure,
Of a life well-lived, of hidden treasure.

JACK

In days of yore, when avarice reigned supreme,
A man named Jack, his heart consumed by dreams,
Of wealth and status, he did strive to gleam,
And so, he chased a fortune, night and beam.

He scrimped and saved, and invested with glee,
But found that all his riches brought was misery,
For though his coffers burst with gold and gem,
His soul grew barren, empty, and forlorn within.

One day, as he lay on his deathbed, weak and worn,
He realized the error of his dawn,
That true wealth lies not in glittering stones or gold,
But in the love of family, and friends so bold.

So let us learn from this cautionary tale,
That chasing false riches will only fail,
For in our hearts, lies the true measure,
Of a life well-lived, of hidden treasure.

In the tapestry of life, Jack's story unfolds,
A tale of heedless pursuit, of treasures untold,
Driven by desire, blinded by greed's allure,
He lost sight of what truly mattered, that was pure.

His days were consumed by a relentless chase,
Of wealth and status, a never-ending race,

But as his coffers grew, his spirit grew thin,
His heart grew cold, devoid of joy within.

For what is wealth if it cannot bring delight?
If it cannot fill the void in the darkest night?
Jack's diamonds and gold, mere trinkets of despair,
A hollow existence, beyond repair.

As time slipped through his fingers like sand,
Jack pondered the worth of riches in his hand,
And on his deathbed, with a heavy sigh,
He realized the truth, as tears filled his eye.

True wealth lies not in material gain,
But in the bonds we forge, the love we sustain,
In the laughter shared, in a warm embrace,
In the memories cherished, time cannot erase.

For family and friends, they are the true gold,
Their love, a treasure that can never be sold,
In their embrace, lies the wealth of a lifetime,
A priceless fortune, a treasure so sublime.

So let us heed Jack's cautionary tale,
And learn from his mistakes before we fail,
For in the pursuit of riches, we may lose sight,
Of the precious moments that make life bright.

In days of yore, when avarice reigned supreme,
Let us remember Jack's quest, his shattered dream,

And choose a path that leads us to the heart,
Where true riches reside, never to depart.

IN DAYS OF YORE REVISITED

In days of yore, when avarice reigned supreme,

A man named Jack, his heart consumed by dreams,

Of wealth and status, he did strive to gleam,

And so, he chased a fortune, night and beam.

He scrimped and saved, and invested with glee,

But found that all his riches brought was misery,

For though his coffers burst with gold and gem,

His soul grew barren, empty, and forlorn within.

One day, as he lay on his deathbed, weak and worn,

He realized the error of his dawn,

That true wealth lies not in glittering stones or gold,

But in the love of family, and friends so bold.

So let us learn from this cautionary tale,

That chasing false riches will only fail,

For in our hearts, lies the true measure,

Of a life well-lived, of hidden treasure.

Midnight Musings: A Poet's Journey

In the depths of night, when all is still and hushed,
My fingers dance upon the keyboard's keys,
A symphony of thoughts, a soul's outburst,
In this vast realm where solitude decrees.

Through the midnight bell, my journey unfolds,
A pilgrimage of words, a sacred quest,
A tapestry of tales, both new and old,
In this nocturnal haven, I am blessed.

I type, embracing darkness as my guide,
With every stroke, my spirit takes its flight,
Through realms unknown, where dreams and visions hide,
I carry on typing through the midnight plight.

For in this solitary realm I dwell,
Unleashing my thoughts, my stories to tell.

As shadows stretch and whisper their refrain,
I weave my verses, crafting every line,
With every click, a piece of me remains,
Embedded in each word, a love divine.

Through the midnight hell, I find my release,
In this nocturnal sanctuary, I'm free,

The keys beneath my fingertips don't cease,
Transcribing thoughts that yearn to be set free.

The ink of night spills onto the white screen,
A dance of letters, forming tales untold,
With every keystroke, a new world convenes,
Where dreams and fantasies forever hold.

For in this realm, my words become a spell,
Transforming darkness into stories large,
As midnight whispers secrets I can't tell,
I carry on typing, forging my charge.

So, let the midnight bell forever chime,
As I embark upon this poet's climb.

Greed's Gilded Epoch: Avarice's Reign Unveiled

In days of yore, when avarice did reign

A golden age for greed, a gilded refrain

The world was mine, or so it seemed to be

As wealth and power, my heart's sole decree

The finest feasts, the rarest treasures sought

My every whim, a kingdom's worth, brought forth

From courts to castles, palaces to halls

My reach was long, my grasp, unlimited walls

But as I gazed upon my glittering throne

I saw not love, nor joy, nor peace alone

For in my quest for more, I lost what's true

And left behind, a trail of hearts, anew

The once-green fields, now barren, dry

The rivers choked, their waters nigh

The skies grew gray, the winds did howl

As nature wept, my legacy unfold

Yet still I craved, my thirst unquenched

My hunger for more, forever unsated

Until one day, my final breath

Did whisper truths, my soul had never heard

That true riches lie within, not gold

That love and kindness, are the greatest wealth to hold

That greed's gilded epoch, but a fleeting dream

And in its wake, only emptiness and screams

So let this tale, be a lesson learned

Of the dangers of avarice, that gnaws and burns

For in the end, it is not gold or wealth

That makes us great, but our own self-worth

A SYMPHONY OF BEAUTY

. Morning sunshine, moonlight skies,
A tapestry of colours, a breathtaking surprise.
Golden rays kissing the earth's embrace,
While the moon retreats, leaving no trace.

The sky, a canvas of infinite hues,
Brushstrokes of warmth, nature's muse.
Vibrant oranges and pinks collide,
As the day awakens, the world comes alive.

Beneath this vast celestial dome,
The beauty of morning finds its home.
Birds serenade with melodies sweet,
Their songs a symphony, a harmony complete.

The air dances with a gentle touch,
Whispering secrets, revealing so much.
Dew-kissed petals, glistening with grace,
Nature's masterpiece, in this sacred space.

The sun ascends, casting light upon all,
Illuminating the world, both big and small.
Shadows retreat, surrendering to the day,
As morning unfolds, in its glorious display.

The moon, a silent observer in the sky,
Waning now, as the sun takes its high.
But still, its presence lingers above,
A reminder of dreams, of hope and of love.

Morning sunshine, moonlight skies,
A symphony of beauty, a visual surprise.
In this vast expanse, we find solace and peace,
As nature's grandeur, our senses release.

Embrace the morning, let its magic unfold,
As the sun and moon, their stories are told.
For in this vast celestial tapestry we roam,
We find beauty, wonder, and a place we call home.

April Falls

Leaves of gold dance on the breeze,
Whispering secrets from ancient trees.
Colours like fire paint the sky,
As nature's canvas comes alive.

In this realm where time suspends,
A symphony of hues transcends.
Each leaf pirouettes with grace,
A ballet performed at nature's pace.

The wind, a gentle conductor's hand,
Guides the leaves in a waltzing band.
They twirl and spin, their golden gowns,
Creating magic in the air, unbound.

With every step, they rustle and sing,
Echoing the wisdom the trees bring.
Stories etched in their veins so old,
Whispered tales from a time untold.

These leaves, once mere adornments fair,
Now become messengers of the air.
They carry secrets from distant years,
Whispering truths that dispel all fears.

The sun, a spotlight in the sky,

Illuminates this dance from high.
Its golden rays illuminate the stage,
Where nature's artistry takes centre stage.

As day turns to dusk, the dance remains,
A spectacle that forever sustains.
Leaves of gold, like embers aglow,
Painting the world in a vibrant show.

So, let us pause and behold this sight,
A masterpiece woven in golden light.
For in this dance, we find solace and peace,
As leaves of gold whisper, never to cease.

THIER WAS A TIME

In days of yore, when tales were told

And legends lived and breathed in gold,

There was a time that I could tell

A story of a magical spell,

Of Triers, where wisdom did abide,

Where truth and dreams intertwined.

In this enchanted land of old,

I found a place where hearts were bold,

Where courage mixed with magic spells,

And love and wonder never fell.

Triers, oh Triers, fair and bright,

Your light still shines like stars at night.

In forests deep and mountains high,

The ancient lore did whisper by,

Of secrets kept and mysteries untold,

That only those who dared to hold,

Could hear the whispers of the earth,

And feel the pulse of life's rebirth.

The rivers flowed with crystal grace,

Reflecting visions of the human race,

Whose footsteps echoed through the halls,

Of knowledge hidden from the walls,

For Triers held the key to all,

To unlock the chambers of the mind,

And find the treasures left behind.

But now, alas, that time is past,

And Triers sleeps beneath the mast,

Yet memories remain, so clear and bright,

Of the wonders that took flight,

In that enchanted land of old,

Where triers once did unfold.

Printed in Great Britain
by Amazon

d3b0cbfb-4b74-40f9-b2db-d26a6823f138R01